The Women's Institute

the**WI**
INSPIRING WOMEN

homemade
soups

SIMON &
SCHUSTER
ILLUSTRATED

London · New York · Sydney · Toronto · New Delhi

A CBS COMPANY

Grace Mulligan
& Dilwen Phillips

First published in Great Britain by
Simon & Schuster UK Ltd, 2012
A CBS Company

Simon & Schuster Illustrated Books,
Simon & Schuster UK Ltd,
222 Gray's Inn Road, London WC1X 8HB

www.simonandschuster.co.uk

Simon & Schuster Australia, Sydney
Simon & Schuster India, New Delhi

1 3 5 7 9 10 8 6 4 2

Editorial Director: **Francine Lawrence**
Senior Commissioning Editor: **Nicky Hill**
Project Editor: **Nicki Lampon**
Designer: **Richard Proctor**
Photographer: **William Shaw**
Stylist and Art Direction: **Tony Hutchinson**
Home Economist: **Sara Lewis**
Commercial Director: **Ami Richards**
Production Manager: **Katherine Thornton**

Colour reproduction by Dot Gradations Ltd, UK

Printed and bound in China

A CIP catalogue record for this book is available
from the British Library

ISBN 978-1-47110-176-2

Notes on the recipes

Both metric and imperial measurements have
been given in all recipes. Use one set of
measurements only and not a mixture of both.
Spoon measures are level and 1 tablespoon =
15 ml, 1 teaspoon = 5 ml.

Preheat ovens before use and cook on the centre
shelf unless cooking more than one item. If using
a fan oven, reduce the heat by 10–20°C, but
check with your handbook.

Medium eggs have been used unless otherwise
stated.

This book contains recipes made with nuts.
Those with known allergic reactions to nuts and
nut derivatives, pregnant and breast-feeding
women and very young children should avoid
these dishes.

Recipes in this book were first published in 2002
under the title *Best-kept Secrets of the Women's
Institute: Soups*.

Contents

Introduction

Coming from Scotland, Grace thinks soup is pretty special. It will often lift your spirits on a dreary day, or even on a sunny one if you aren't feeling special yourself. The stories of Jewish mothers who cure everything with chicken soup have something to them!

The soups Dilwen's mother made were from home-grown vegetables, herbs and meat in season and, when needed, dried pulses and home-cured ham and bacon. They certainly did not have available the range of ingredients that is in this book. Soup is still important in her household, taken mainly as a light lunch, and her grandchildren enjoy a mug of puréed soup. She finds this is an excellent way of getting them to eat vegetables they might otherwise reject, and the soup colours are appealing.

It's depressing, however, that so many people turn to cans or packets when they think of having soup. Often, one look at the ingredients list will tell you a sad tale of artificial flavours, starches and E numbers. Hopefully, the tasty, user-friendly recipes in this book will tempt you to sample the delights and flavours of our homemade soups.

Hints and tips

Anyone who can cut up fresh vegetables can make soup, and you do not have to spend all morning doing it. If you are really pressed for time, buy a packet of chopped fresh vegetables. Just check that they are really fresh and moist. Almost any vegetable can be made into soup and this is a great way to use up any odd vegetables that are left in the fridge at the end of the week.

Pulses, such as lentils, split peas, dried green peas and chick peas, can make soups really substantial and filling and are a good source of protein. Also, don't forget what a delicious and useful addition potatoes are. White floury potatoes, which break down during cooking, not only add their flavour but are good natural thickeners. Waxy potatoes, on the other hand, give a soup good texture. We underestimate potatoes.

Herbs are important to soups, not just for flavouring but also for their colour. We are generally too mean with herbs. Fresh herbs have been used throughout this book; if you are substituting dried herbs, reduce the quantity by half.

The terms 'sauté', 'sweat' and 'soften' are all used in recipes to describe the initial cooking of onions or vegetables in oil or butter. Basically, they all mean the same thing: the technique softens the onions and/or other vegetables and develops the flavour but without caramelising (that is, without browning). A gentle heat and a covered pan (so the steam is retained to help soften the vegetables) should be used, and you should shake the pan frequently to prevent the contents from sticking and browning. 'Frying', on the other hand, means softening and colouring onions, other vegetables and/or meat. This process adds the flavours developed by caramelising as well as giving colour to the finished dish.

Many soups in this book have been puréed to give a smooth texture. Liquidisers, food processors and hand-held blenders can all be used. A hand-held blender is perhaps the easiest because you can purée the soup while still in the saucepan, saving on washing up. Liquidisers produce the smoothest purée, while a food processor will also produce a perfectly good result if the soup is processed in short bursts.

Most soups can be frozen and, if you are just cooking for one or two, you can have real instant soup in your freezer by making quantities for four or more – which takes just the same time – and freezing portions. Just remember to label and date your containers and use them within 2 months. Dairy products such as cheese can be problematic when frozen but this should not affect these recipes; as long as soups are reheated fairly gently but thoroughly they should be fine; any separation of fat in soups containing cheese or cream can be dispersed with a good whisking.

There are many easy ways to make a soup look extra special. It can be as simple as scattering over a few chopped herbs or a few crunchy croûtons. Croûtons are made by frying cubed bread in a little oil until brown and crisp. You could also consider larger pieces of bread called croûtes. They are either grilled or baked. If the bread is spread lightly with a layer of garlic butter prior to baking it is even better. Grated cheese, toasted on thin slices of French bread, is the classic topping for French Onion Soup (page 82) but is also a nice idea for tomato and fish soups. You could also consider little baked puff pastry shapes for special occasions. Another easy finishing touch is to swirl a spoonful of cream, crème fraîche or natural or Greek style yogurt into each serving of a smooth soup.

Stocks

A while ago, the chef-restaurateur and television presenter Brian Turner gave a demonstration to the Guild of Food Writers, of which Grace is a member. He showed us how stock was made – and still is, at quality restaurants – in the classic tradition. He took us through all the stages and let us taste the liquid as it improved and improved. Even vegetable stock was triumphantly tasty!

Brian used huge, vat-like pans. He showed the group what went into the stock, the vegetables, the bouquet garnis, the veal bones and fish bones. Long, slow cooking, skimming and de-greasing were all part of it. Then the liquid was strained, cooled quickly, and the remaining fat was lifted from the top. At this point the liquid was reheated and cooked again in open pans, to reduce the quantity and strengthen the flavour. The reduction process is often needed to strengthen flavour or just to reduce the quantity of liquid by half so that it takes up less room in the freezer. The quickest

way is to use a wide pan with the lid off over a moderate heat.

Brian's demonstration was superb. He showed us more clearly than ever why good stock is best.

If you make your own stock, the feeling of satisfaction of getting something for nothing may well never leave you! You can also use stock cubes and bouillon powder. It is fair to say that the best is expensive; however, you can often use just half of the stated amount on the label. It is up to you to taste the dish and see. Fresh stock is also available in supermarket chill cabinets. This is extremely good but can be expensive.

Remember that stock cubes and granules contain a percentage of salt. Read the

labels carefully and adjust the salt in the recipe. Do not season stock when you make it. Salt and pepper are best added only when you use the stock for soups and sauces.

When making your own stock, it is important to cool it as quickly as possible by sitting the pan in a sink of cold water until the stock is cool enough to go in the fridge. It can be easily frozen for future use and is best if used within 3 months. Freeze it as soon as possible and label carefully with the type of stock and the date of making.

Finally

Whether you take your soup whizzed to smooth perfection in a mug for a quick lunch, or served in a china bowl on a nicely laid table, do enjoy our recipes and then use them as the basis for trying out your own ideas. In no time at all you will be making up your own soups.

We would like to thank friends and colleagues for sharing their recipes and ideas with us and hope you enjoy cooking and eating the soups.

Vegetable stock

You can use whatever vegetables you have to make this stock, adding any herbs that you are fond of.

**Makes about
1.1 litres (2 pints)
Preparation time:
15 minutes
Cooking time:
30–40 minutes
Freezing:
recommended**

1 small **lemon**, scrubbed
  and chopped roughly
1 thick **celery stick**,
  chopped
2 **carrots**, peeled and
  chopped
1 **onion**, chopped
1 teaspoon whole **black
  peppercorns**
fresh **herbs** (e.g. parsley
  stalks, small bay leaf
  and thyme sprig) or
  ½ teaspoon dried **thyme**
1 small **garlic clove**, sliced
  (optional)

Put everything into a large lidded pan with 1.1 litres (2 pints) of water. Bring to the boil, reduce the heat and leave to simmer for 30–40 minutes with the lid of the pan at an angle. This prevents the stock from boiling over and also helps to reduce the volume and increase the flavour. Any scum that rises to the surface should be skimmed off and discarded.

Strain the stock through a fine sieve and taste. You may wish to reduce it further to strengthen the flavour. If necessary, simmer in an open pan until you are happy with the taste.

Tip Use for soups or sauces or freeze for future use. Remember to label carefully, stating the type of stock and date. Only season the stock when you use it.

Chicken stock

Chicken is probably the most useful stock. Freeze the carcasses until you have enough to make a batch. You can also include skin and jelly.

Makes about
1.1 litres (2 pints)
Preparation time:
10 minutes
Cooking time:
2–2½ hours
Freezing:
recommended

2 large **chicken carcasses**
   or 3 smaller ones
1 large **onion**, sliced
2 **celery sticks**, chopped
1 large **carrot**, peeled and
   chopped
fresh **herbs** (e.g. parsley
   stalks, small bay leaf,
   thyme sprig and tarragon
   sprig) or ½ teaspoon dried
   tarragon
1 fat **garlic clove**, chopped
   (optional)
10 whole **black peppercorns**

Put everything into a large lidded pan (break the carcasses up a bit to fit) with 1.1 litres (2 pints) of water. Bring to the boil, reduce the heat and leave to simmer for 2–2½ hours with the lid of the pan at an angle. This prevents the stock from boiling over and also helps to reduce the volume and increase the flavour. Refrain from boiling hard as this can make the stock cloudy. Any scum that rises to the surface should be skimmed off and discarded.

Strain the stock through a fine sieve and taste. You may wish to reduce it further to strengthen the flavour. If necessary, simmer in an open pan until you are happy with the taste.

Tips Use for soups or sauces or freeze for future use. Before freezing, remove any fat that rises to the surface during cooling. Remember to label carefully, stating the type of stock and date. Only season the stock when you use it.

The colour of this stock is quite light. To make a darker stock, first fry the broken carcasses in oil until they are brown. You can also sear the onion by cutting it in two and frying the cut sides until almost burnt. The resulting stock will be much darker after this treatment. The addition of a glass of dry white wine or even brandy gives another dimension to the flavour. Tarragon is one of Grace's favourite herbs for adding to this stock.

Fish stock

This is very quick to make. You can save white fish bones in the freezer or ask your fishmonger for some. Dry white wine gives it a lovely flavour.

**Makes about
1.1 litres (2 pints)
Preparation time:
10 minutes
Cooking time:
25 minutes
Freezing:
recommended**

900 g (2 lb) **white fish bones**, rinsed
250 ml (9 fl oz) **dry white wine**
115 g (4¼ oz) **white button mushrooms**, sliced
1 small **onion**, sliced
fresh **herbs** (e.g. parsley stalks and tarragon leaves)
5–6 whole **black peppercorns**

Put everything into a large lidded pan with 1.7 litres (3 pints) of water. Bring to the boil, reduce the heat and leave to simmer gently for 20 minutes with the lid of the pan at an angle. This prevents the stock from boiling over and also helps to reduce the volume and increase the flavour. Any scum that rises to the surface should be skimmed off and discarded.

Strain the stock through a fine sieve and taste. You may wish to reduce it further to strengthen the flavour. If necessary, simmer in an open pan until you are happy with the taste.

Tip Use for soups or sauces or freeze for future use. Remember to label carefully, stating the type of stock and date. Only season the stock when you use it.

Beef stock

Store the bones from your Sunday roasts in the freezer and, when you have enough, roast them again in the oven along with some vegetables.

**Makes about
1.1 litres (2 pints)
Preparation time:
15 minutes
Cooking time:
3¼ hours
Freezing:
recommended**

1.3 kg (3 lb) **beef bones** from cooked joints
2 **onions**, topped, tailed and quartered (remove and reserve the skin)
2–3 **celery sticks**, chopped
2 large **carrots**, peeled and chopped
10 whole **black peppercorns**
fresh **herbs** (e.g. parsley stalks, small bay leaf and thyme sprig) or ½ teaspoon dried **thyme**
125 ml (4 fl oz) **red wine** (optional)

First of all, turn the oven to its highest setting. Pack the bones into a large roasting tin, push the onions, celery and carrots in among the bones and roast for about 45 minutes, by which time the bones should have darkened and the vegetables will have softened and scorched just a little.

Transfer the contents of the roasting tin into a large lidded saucepan. Add the onion skins, peppercorns, herbs and 1.7 litres (3 pints) of water. Add the red wine, if using, or a glass of water to the roasting tin and stir vigorously to deglaze the tin and pick up all the flavour. Add the liquid to the saucepan.

Bring to the boil, reduce the heat and leave to simmer for about 2½ hours with the lid of the pan at an angle. This prevents the stock from boiling over and also helps to reduce the volume and increase the flavour. Any scum that rises to the surface should be skimmed off and discarded.

Strain the stock through a fine sieve and taste. You may wish to reduce it further to strengthen the flavour. If necessary, simmer in an open pan until you are happy with the taste.

Tips Meat stock needs to be dark in colour. Use for soups or sauces or freeze for future use. Before freezing, remove any fat that rises to the surface during cooling. Remember to label carefully, stating the type of stock and date. Only season the stock when you use it.

A fair substitute for homemade beef stock is a can of beef consommé, which you can dilute a bit to extend it.

Cream of watercress

A wonderful vibrant green colour, this is best made in spring when watercress is at its best.

Serves 4
**Preparation and
  cooking time:
  40 minutes**
**Freezing:
  not recommended**

25 g (1 oz) **butter**
1 **onion**, chopped
2 bunches **watercress**,
  washed and chopped
  roughly
40 g (1½ oz) **plain flour**
850 ml (1½ pints) **chicken
  stock** (see page 9)
150 ml (5 fl oz) **single cream**
salt and freshly ground
  black pepper
a little freshly grated
  nutmeg

Melt the butter in a large lidded saucepan. Add the onion and sweat, covered, shaking the pan from time to time, until softened but not browned.

Add the watercress, reserving a few leaves to garnish if wished. Cover again and allow to sweat for 10 minutes.

Stir in the flour and cook for 1 minute. Add the stock, stirring well to ensure the flour is well blended, and then bring to the boil. Reduce to a simmer and cook for 5 minutes.

Remove the soup from the heat and leave to cool briefly. Blend until smooth. Stir in half of the cream, adjust the seasoning if necessary and add a little nutmeg to taste. Reheat gently.

Serve garnished with a swirl of the remaining cream and the reserved watercress leaves, if using.

Scallop chowder

The name 'chowder' comes from the French *chaudière*, a large cooking pan. Use any combination of available fish and vegetables to suit your taste.

Serves 4
Preparation time:
  30 minutes
Cooking time:
  15–20 minutes
Freezing:
  not recommended

125 g (4½ oz) rindless
  streaky bacon, chopped
1 large **onion**, chopped
350 g (12 oz) **potatoes**,
  peeled and chopped
1 **carrot**, peeled and
  chopped
1 small **parsnip**, peeled and
  chopped
425 ml (15 fl oz) **fish stock**
  (see page 10)
8 **scallops**
juice of a **lemon**
25 g (1 oz) **plain flour**
600 ml (20 fl oz)
  semi-skimmed milk
salt and freshly ground
  black pepper
1 tablespoon chopped fresh
  parsley, to garnish

Heat a large lidded saucepan and dry fry the bacon over a low heat until the fat is released. Add the onion and sweat, covered, shaking the pan from time to time, until softened but not browned.

Add the remaining vegetables and the stock. Bring to the boil and then reduce the heat and simmer for 15–20 minutes, or until the vegetables are cooked.

Meanwhile, wash the scallops and set the corals aside. Roughly chop the white flesh and sprinkle with the lemon juice.

Blend the flour with a little of the milk until smooth. Add the remainder of the milk and then pour the mixture into the vegetables. Stir until the soup has thickened.

Add the chopped scallops and simmer for 5 minutes. Add the corals and simmer for 2 minutes. Taste and adjust the seasoning if necessary. Serve sprinkled with the parsley.

Butternut squash & apple

Butternut squash is available from autumn through to spring. The combination of flavours makes a delicious soup.

Serves 4
Preparation time:
  25 minutes
Cooking time:
  15–20 minutes
Freezing:
  recommended

1 tablespoon **vegetable** or
  olive oil
1 **onion**, sliced thinly
1 teaspoon **curry powder**
2 **eating apples**, peeled,
  cored and chopped
1 **butternut squash**, peeled,
  de-seeded and chopped
1 litre (1¾ pints) **vegetable
  stock** (see page 8)
salt and freshly ground
  black pepper
Croûtons, to garnish (see
  page 30)

Heat the oil in a large lidded saucepan. Add the onion and sweat, covered, for 4–5 minutes, shaking the pan from time to time, until softened but not browned.

Stir in the curry powder and apple and cook for 2 minutes.

Add the squash and stock. Bring to the boil and then reduce the heat. Simmer for 15–20 minutes.

Remove the soup from the heat and leave to cool briefly. Blend until smooth. Adjust the seasoning if necessary and then reheat gently. Thin the soup with a little more stock, if wished. Serve scattered with the croûtons.

Cauliflower & broccoli

The addition of walnuts gives this cheesy vegetable soup an interesting crunchy texture.

Serves 4
Preparation and cooking time:
25 minutes
Freezing:
recommended, before adding cheeses

1 tablespoon **sunflower oil**
1 small **onion**, chopped
350 g (12 oz) **cauliflower florets**
350 g (12 oz) **broccoli florets**
1.1 litres (2 pints) **vegetable stock** (see page 8)
25 g (1 oz) **plain flour**
30 ml (1 fl oz) **semi-skimmed milk**
25 g (1 oz) **walnuts**, chopped
½ teaspoon freshly grated **nutmeg**
200 g (7 oz) **cream cheese**
115 g (4¼ oz) **mature Cheddar cheese**, grated
salt and freshly ground **black pepper**
Croûtons, to serve (see page 30)

Heat the oil in a large lidded saucepan. Add the onion and sweat, covered, shaking the pan from time to time, until softened but not browned.

Add the cauliflower, broccoli and stock. Cook for 5–10 minutes; the cauliflower and broccoli should be tender but not soft.

Blend the flour and milk together and add to the cauliflower and broccoli. Add the walnuts and nutmeg.

Add the two cheeses and stir the soup over a gentle heat until the cheese is well blended and the soup has thickened. Adjust the seasoning. Serve scattered with the croûtons.

Celery, apple & Stilton

The sharpness of the apple counteracts the richness of the cheese in this unusual soup.

Serves 4
Preparation time:
 20 minutes
Cooking time:
 20 minutes
Freezing:
 recommended, before adding cheese

25 g (1 oz) **butter**
1 **onion**, chopped
3 **celery sticks**, chopped
1 tablespoon **plain flour**
600 ml (20 fl oz) **vegetable stock** (see page 8)
150 ml (5 fl oz) **white wine**
300 ml (10 fl oz)
 semi-skimmed milk
1 **bay leaf**
½ teaspoon dried **mixed herbs**
1 **cooking apple**, peeled, cored and chopped
80 g (3 oz) **Stilton cheese**, diced finely
salt and freshly ground **black pepper**
Croûtons (see page 30), to serve

Melt the butter in a large lidded saucepan. Add the onion and celery and sweat for 2–3 minutes, covered, shaking the pan from time to time, until softened but not browned.

Stir in the flour and cook for a further minute. Gradually add the stock and wine. Bring to the boil, stirring, until thickened.

Add the milk, bay leaf, herbs and apple. Bring back to the boil, cover and simmer for 20 minutes.

Remove the soup from the heat and leave to cool briefly. Remove the bay leaf and blend the soup until smooth.

Add the cheese and heat gently until the cheese has melted. Adjust the seasoning if necessary. Serve scattered with the croûtons.

Red pepper & goat's cheese

This creamy soup is a delicious blend of flavours enriched by the addition of goat's cheese. Everyone who's tried it agrees that it is moreish.

Serves 6
Preparation time:
 20 minutes
Cooking time:
 20 minutes
Freezing:
 recommended, before adding cheese

2 **onions**, chopped
1.7 litres (3 pints) **vegetable stock** (see page 8)
60 ml (2½ fl oz) **dry white wine**
8 **red peppers**, de-seeded and chopped
1 large **cooking apple**, cored and chopped
1 teaspoon chopped fresh **basil**, plus 12 tiny leaves, to garnish
salt and freshly ground **black pepper**
150 g (5½ oz) **goat's cheese**, rind removed, diced
olive oil, to garnish

In a large saucepan, boil the onions in a little of the stock until the stock has evaporated and the onions are beginning to caramelise.

Add the remaining stock, wine, peppers, apple and chopped basil. Cook over a low heat for 20 minutes.

Remove the soup from the heat and leave to cool briefly. Blend until smooth. Adjust the seasoning if necessary and then reheat gently. Add half of the cheese and whisk over a gentle heat until blended.

Serve garnished with the remaining cheese, tiny basil leaves, a drizzle of olive oil and a grinding of black pepper.

Tasty cabbage

No soup book would be complete without cabbage soup, and this is an excellent way of using a glut of cabbage from the garden.

Serves 8
Preparation:
   20 minutes
Cooking time:
   25–30 minutes
Freezing:
   recommended

6 large **onions**, chopped
2 large **green peppers**,
   de-seeded and chopped
1 head **celery**, chopped
2 x 400 g cans **tomatoes**
40 g (1½ oz) **tomato purée**
hot **vegetable stock** (see
   page 8)
1 green **cabbage**, shredded

Flavourings
(use some of the following)
1 **lemongrass stem**
3 **garlic cloves**, crushed
7.5 cm (3 inches) fresh **root
   ginger**, grated
2 teaspoons **caraway seeds**
dried **mixed herbs**
2 **chillies**, de-seeded and
   sliced thinly

Put the onions, peppers, celery, tomatoes and tomato purée into a large saucepan. Add enough boiling stock to come halfway up the vegetables.

Add any flavourings you like, bring to the boil and simmer for about 20 minutes. Add the cabbage and cook for a further 5–10 minutes. If necessary, top up with extra stock once the cabbage has been added. Serve.

Tip Other vegetables can also be added to provide variety – try courgettes, beansprouts, fennel or spinach.

Cullen skink

Skink means 'stock' or 'broth', while Cullen is the name of a fishing village in Aberdeenshire. This is a traditional Scottish soup and a meal in itself.

Serves 4
Preparation and
** cooking time:**
** 50 minutes**
Freezing:
** not recommended**

350 g (12 oz) **Finnan**
  haddock (see Tips)
1 **onion**, chopped
1 small **carrot**, peeled and
  chopped
4 whole **cloves**
850 ml (1½ pints) **fish stock**
  (see page 10) or **water**
600 ml (20 fl oz)
  semi-skimmed milk
450 g (1 lb) **potatoes**, peeled
  and chopped roughly
25 g (1 oz) **butter**
salt and freshly ground
  black pepper
chopped fresh **parsley**,
  to garnish

Put the haddock, onion, carrot and cloves in a pan and pour over the water or stock. Bring gently to the boil and simmer for no more than 5 minutes.

Remove the fish and, when cool enough to handle, remove the skin and bones. Return the skin and bones to the pan, add the milk and continue cooking over a low heat. Flake the haddock flesh into a bowl.

Meanwhile, bring a second pan of water to the boil and cook the potatoes until tender. Drain, leaving a little water in the pan, and then mash with the butter.

Strain the milky stock from the fish bones and vegetables and blend into the mashed potatoes until the mixture is smooth. Add the flaked haddock.

Reheat the soup without boiling, but be careful not to overcook it. Adjust the seasoning. Serve garnished with the parsley.

Tips The authentic recipe uses Finnan haddock (a particular type of smoked haddock) but, if you can't get this, choose a haddock that is smoked but not dyed. Remember that fish should not be cooked for too long, otherwise it becomes tough.

Two pans are needed for this soup, unless you cook the potatoes beforehand.

Cream of lemon

This is the ideal starter for a meal with a substantial main course because it is light and fresh, with the slight sharpness of the lemon.

Serves 4
Preparation time:
 20 minutes
Cooking time:
 15 minutes
Freezing:
 recommended, before adding lemon juice

25 g (1 oz) **butter**
2 **onions**, chopped finely
80 g (3 oz) **carrots**, peeled and grated
80 g (3 oz) **celery**, chopped very finely
2 **lemons**
15 g (½ oz) **plain flour**
1.1 litres (2 pints) **chicken stock** (see page 9)
2 **bay leaves**
salt and freshly ground **black pepper**
150 ml (5 fl oz) **single cream**, to serve

Melt the butter in a large lidded saucepan. Add the onions, carrots and celery and sweat over a low heat for 10–15 minutes, covered, shaking the pan from time to time, until softened but not browned.

Remove some strips of lemon zest (with a zester if available) and reserve for the garnish. Grate the remaining zest from both lemons and squeeze out the juice. Set both aside.

Add the flour to the vegetables in the pan, mix well and cook briefly. Stir in the chicken stock, making sure the flour has blended smoothly. Add the bay leaves and grated lemon zest. Cook for 15 minutes or until the vegetables are soft.

Remove the bay leaves and add 4 teaspoons of the lemon juice. Adjust the seasoning and add more lemon juice to taste if necessary. Stir in the cream and reheat gently, without boiling. Serve garnished with the reserved strips of lemon zest.

Tip This soup can be blended until smooth if you prefer.

Chicken & barley broth

Barley has long been included in traditional soups. It gives great texture and is, happily, making something of a comeback.

Serves 4
Preparation time:
 20 minutes
Cooking time:
 2 hours
Freezing:
 not recommended

1 tablespoon **vegetable** or **olive oil**
4 **chicken drumsticks**
1 **onion**, chopped finely
1 **carrot**, peeled and chopped finely
1 **celery stick**, chopped finely
2 **potatoes**, peeled and chopped finely
1 **leek**, sliced finely, white and green parts separated
1.1 litres (2 pints) **chicken stock** (see page 9)
40 g (1½ oz) **pearl barley**
1 **bay leaf**
1 fresh **thyme sprig**
4 tablespoons chopped fresh **parsley**
salt and freshly ground **black pepper**

Using a large lidded saucepan, heat the oil over a high heat and fry the drumsticks until they are well browned all over. Use tongs to remove the chicken to a plate and set aside. Lower the heat a little.

Add the onion, carrot, celery, potatoes and white part of the leek to the pan and sweat the vegetables for about 10 minutes, covered, shaking the pan from time to time until the vegetables are softened but not browned (you may need to add a little more oil).

Add the stock, pearl barley, herbs and chicken. Bring to the boil and then reduce the heat to a simmer. Cook for about 2 hours, stirring often. Add the green part of the leek for the last 5 minutes of cooking time (this helps to preserve the green colour).

Remove the chicken to a plate and fish out the bay leaf and thyme sprig. When the chicken is cool enough to handle, separate the meat from the skin and bones. Chop the meat and return it to the broth. Adjust the seasoning and serve.

Curried coconut vegetable

Do not be put off by the list of ingredients in this soup – it is so unusual and delicious that it is worth making the effort!

Serves 6–8
**Preparation and
  cooking time:
  1 hour**
**Freezing:
  recommended**

50 g (1¾ oz) **butter**
seeds from 3 green
  cardamom pods (see Tip)
1 teaspoon **ground coriander**
1 teaspoon **ground cumin**
a large pinch of **turmeric**
2 large **carrots**, peeled and
  chopped
2 **leeks**, chopped
225 g (8 oz) **celeriac**, peeled
  and chopped, or 4 thick
  celery sticks, chopped
3 thick **lemongrass stems**,
  chopped
1 fat **garlic clove**, grated
  coarsely
2.5 cm (1 inch) fresh **root
  ginger**, grated
400 ml can **coconut milk**
1.1 litres (2 pints) **chicken
  stock** (see page 9)
salt and freshly ground
  black pepper

Melt the butter in a large lidded saucepan and fry the cardamom seeds, coriander, cumin and turmeric. Keep the heat low.

Add all the vegetables, lemongrass, garlic and ginger and stir well. Cover and sweat them for a few minutes, shaking often.

Stir in the coconut milk and stock. Bring to the boil and then reduce the heat and leave to simmer for about 30 minutes or until the vegetables are soft.

Blend until smooth and then pour through a nylon sieve into a clean pan. Adjust the seasoning if necessary and then reheat gently. Serve.

Tip To prepare the cardamom pods, roughly crush with the end of a rolling pin or with a pestle and mortar and extract the seeds. Discard the pods.

Green pea, ham & leek

This is a substantial, satisfying soup with a very good flavour and is ideal for lunch on a cold day.

Serves 4
Preparation time:
  25 minutes
Cooking time:
  15 minutes
Freezing:
  recommended, before
  adding ham

1 tablespoon **vegetable**
  or **olive oil**
3 **leeks**, sliced
175 g (6 oz) **frozen peas**
850 ml (1½ pints) **chicken**
  stock (see page 9)
175 g (6 oz) **ham**, cut into
  chunks
2 tablespoons chopped
  fresh **mint**
150 ml (5 fl oz) **double**
  cream, to serve

Heat the oil in a large lidded saucepan. Add the leeks and sweat for 8 minutes, covered, shaking the pan from time to time, until softened but not browned.

Add the peas and stock and bring to the boil. Cover and simmer for 15 minutes.

Remove the soup from the heat and leave to cool briefly. Blend until coarse. Stir in the ham and mint and reheat gently. Serve garnished with a swirl of cream.

Tip For extra taste, use a thick slice of the best quality ham you can get.

Cream of mushroom

This is a classic cream of mushroom recipe with the addition of tasty little croûtons to give it a crunch.

Serves 4
Preparation and cooking time:
40 minutes
Freezing:
recommended

50 g (1¾ oz) **butter**
450 g (1 lb) **mushrooms**, chopped finely
1 **onion**, chopped finely
1 **garlic clove**, crushed (optional)
25 g (1 oz) **plain flour**
450 ml (16 fl oz) **semi-skimmed milk**
450 ml (16 fl oz) **vegetable** or **chicken stock** (see pages 8 or 9)
salt and freshly ground **black pepper**
150 ml (5 fl oz) **double cream**

Croûtons
(optional)
olive oil
1 thick slice day-old **white bread**, crusts removed, cubed

Melt the butter in a large lidded saucepan. Add the mushrooms, onion and garlic, if using, and sweat, covered, shaking the pan from time to time, until softened but not browned. Remove a few of the mushrooms and reserve for the garnish.

Add the flour and stir in well. Cook briefly. Add the milk and stock and stir well to make sure the flour is completely blended. Bring to the boil and simmer for 15 minutes.

Meanwhile, make the croûtons. Heat the olive oil and fry the cubes of bread over a brisk heat for a few minutes until browned on all sides. Remove with a slotted spoon and place on kitchen towel to dry. Keep warm.

Remove the soup from the heat and leave to cool briefly. Blend until smooth. Adjust the seasoning if necessary and then reheat gently.

Serve garnished with a swirl of cream, the reserved mushrooms, a grinding of black pepper and the croûtons, if using.

Tip For an extra garnish, fry some sliced chestnut mushrooms in a little butter.

Salmon & dill

This is a lovely soup for a special occasion – rich and creamy and one to impress your friends.

Serves 4–5
Preparation time:
10 minutes
Cooking time:
10 minutes
Freezing:
not recommended

25 g (1 oz) **butter**
1 **onion**, chopped
50 g (1¾ oz) **plain flou**r
700 ml (1¼ pints) **fish stock**
   (see page 10)
450 g (1 lb) **tomatoes**,
   skinned and chopped
   roughly, or 400 g can
   chopped tomatoes
2 x 150 g (5½ oz) **salmon**
   fillets
1 tablespoon chopped fresh
   dill, plus extra sprigs, to
   garnish
2 teaspoons **lemon juice**
150 ml (5 fl oz) **double cream**
80 ml (3 fl oz) **white wine**
salt and freshly ground
   black pepper
curls of zest from ½ a **lemon**

Melt the butter in a large lidded saucepan. Add the onion and sweat for 5 minutes, covered, shaking the pan from time to time, until softened but not browned.

Add the flour and cook, stirring, for a further minute. Stir in the fish stock, making sure the flour is well blended.

Add the tomatoes and salmon. Bring to the boil, cover and simmer for 10 minutes.

Lift the salmon from the pan, remove the skin and flake the flesh, discarding any bones. Set aside.

Remove the soup from the heat and leave to cool briefly. Blend until smooth. Add the dill, lemon juice, cream and wine. Adjust the seasoning if necessary and then reheat gently.

Serve in shallow bowls, topped with the flaked salmon and garnished with the sprigs of dill, lemon zest and a grinding of black pepper.

Asparagus & pea

This soup is also delicious made with canned asparagus and frozen peas, so it can be enjoyed at any time of year.

Serves 4
Preparation and cooking time:
  40 minutes
Freezing:
  not recommended

850 ml (1½ pints) **chicken stock** (see page 9)
450 g (1 lb) **asparagus spears**
225 g (8 oz) shelled fresh **peas**
1 fresh **mint sprig**
40 g (1½ oz) **butter**, melted
40 g (1½ oz) **plain flour**
300 ml (10 fl oz) **semi-skimmed milk**
salt and freshly ground **black pepper**
4 tablespoons **single cream**, to serve

Put the stock, asparagus, peas and mint into a large saucepan. Bring to the boil and simmer for 10–15 minutes, until tender.

Meanwhile, blend the butter and flour together. Bring the milk to the boil in a second saucepan and whisk walnut-sized pieces of the blended butter and flour into the milk until smooth. Continue cooking until the sauce has thickened.

Remove the soup from the heat and leave to cool briefly. Blend until smooth. Add the sauce to the blended soup and mix together. Adjust the seasoning if necessary and then reheat gently. Serve garnished with a swirl of cream.

Roasted pepper & tomato

An interesting soup with a lovely colour and flavour. It can be served either hot or cold.

Serves 4
Preparation time:
  25 minutes
Cooking time:
  45 minutes
Freezing:
  recommended

4 **red peppers**, halved
  lengthways and
  de-seeded
6 ripe **tomatoes**, skinned
  (see Tip) and halved
1 tablespoon **olive oil**
1 teaspoon **caster sugar**
1 tablespoon chopped
  fresh **basil**, plus extra
  to garnish
1 **onion**, chopped finely
1 **garlic clove**, crushed
600 ml (20 fl oz) **vegetable
  stock** (see page 8)
salt and freshly ground
  black pepper

Preheat the oven to 190°C/375°F/Gas Mark 5.

Place the peppers, skin-side up, and the tomatoes, cut-side up, on a baking tray. Drizzle with half the oil and sprinkle with the sugar and chopped basil. Roast in the oven for 30 minutes.

Meanwhile, in a large lidded saucepan, sweat the onion and garlic in the remaining oil, covered, shaking the pan from time to time, until softened but not browned.

As soon as they are cool enough to handle, remove the skins from the peppers. Add the peppers, tomatoes and any juices to the saucepan, cover with the stock and bring to the boil. Turn down the heat and simmer for 15 minutes.

Remove the soup from the heat and leave to cool briefly. Blend until smooth. Adjust the seasoning if necessary and then reheat gently. Serve garnished with the extra chopped basil.

Tip To skin tomatoes, put them in a bowl and pour boiling water over them to cover. Leave for a minute or two and then make a small slit at one end and slip the skins off.

Green pea & cabbage

If you live in an area where peas are grown in quantity, try blanching and freezing them – and keep an eye open for good recipes.

Serves 4–6
Preparation and cooking time: 40 minutes
Freezing: recommended

150 g (5½ oz) **butter**
350 g (12 oz) fresh shelled or frozen **peas**
675 g (1 lb 8 oz) **spring greens** or **Savoy cabbage**, chopped finely and coarse stems discarded
600 ml (20 fl oz) **vegetable** or **chicken stock** (see pages 8 or 9)
1 teaspoon **caster sugar**
2 teaspoons **salt**
freshly ground **black pepper**

Melt 50 g (2 oz) of the butter in a large lidded saucepan and stir in the peas and 150 ml (5 fl oz) of water. Simmer for 2–3 minutes or until the peas are cooked.

Remove the soup from the heat and leave to cool briefly. Blend until smooth.

Empty the pea mixture into a bowl and wash the pan. Melt the rest of the butter and stir in the cabbage. Cook gently, covered, shaking the pan from time to time, until the cabbage is softened but not browned.

Stir in the stock, sugar, salt and 275 ml (10 fl oz) of water. Simmer until the cabbage is well cooked – about 5–10 minutes.

Remove the soup from the heat and leave to cool briefly. Blend until the cabbage is almost reduced to a purée.

Stir the pea purée into the cabbage. Reheat gently. Serve garnished with a rough grinding of black pepper.

Borscht

Borscht is originally from the Ukraine, but it has become popular in many Eastern and Central European countries and right around the world.

Serves 4
Preparation time:
  15 minutes
Cooking time:
  45–60 minutes
Freezing:
  recommended

1 large **onion**, grated
1 large **potato**, peeled and
  grated
450 g (1 lb) raw **beetroot**,
  peeled and grated
300 ml (10 fl oz) **tomato juice**
600 ml (20 fl oz) **vegetable
  stock** (see page 8) or
  water
1 teaspoon **caraway seeds**
salt and freshly ground
  black pepper
a little freshly grated
  nutmeg

To garnish
150 g (5½ oz) **crème fraîche**
  or **natural yogurt**
snipped fresh **dill**

Put all the vegetables in a large lidded saucepan and add the tomato juice, stock or water and caraway seeds. Bring to the boil, cover and simmer for 45–60 minutes. Season to taste with salt, pepper and nutmeg.

Serve as a coarsely textured soup or cool briefly and then blend until smooth.

Serve hot or cold, garnished with a generous spoonful of crème fraîche or yogurt, a little dill and a grinding of black pepper.

Chinese pak choi & noodles

This clear soup full of vegetables and noodles is typically Chinese. Chestnut mushrooms are ideal because they stay fairly firm and have a good flavour.

Serves 4
Preparation and cooking time: 20 minutes
Freezing: recommended

1 litre (1¾ pints) **chicken stock** (see page 9)
1 teaspoon finely chopped fresh **root ginger**
1 small **red chilli**, de-seeded and chopped finely
juice of ½ a **lime**
1 tablespoon **light soy sauce**
50 g (1¾ oz) **chestnut mushrooms**
2 **pak choi heads**, finely sliced
150 g (5½ oz) dried **fine thread egg noodles**
a kettle full of **boiling water**
2 tablespoons chopped fresh **coriander**

Put the stock, ginger, chilli, lime juice and light soy sauce in a large saucepan. Simmer for 5 minutes over a moderate heat.

Stir in the mushrooms and pak choi and continue cooking for another 5–7 minutes or until the green stems are cooked but not soggy.

Place the noodles in a bowl and pour boiling water over them. Stir to separate the strands and then leave to soak according to the packet instructions. Drain off the water and divide the wet noodles between four warm bowls.

Top up with the soup and decorate each bowl with chopped coriander.

Leek, potato & lavender

Flowers and herbs give soups a unique flavour – lavender has been used in cooking for many years. It is fairly pungent, so do not use too much.

Serves 4–6
Preparation time:
 30 minutes
Cooking time:
 30 minutes
Freezing:
 recommended

1 tablespoon **vegetable** or
 olive oil
2 **leeks**, chopped, white and
 green parts separated
450 g (1 lb) **potatoes**, peeled
 and chopped
850 ml (1½ pints) **vegetable
 stock** (see page 8)
300 ml (10 fl oz)
 semi-skimmed milk
6 **lavender sprigs**, tied in
 a piece of muslin, plus
 a few petals, to garnish
salt and freshly ground
 black pepper
4–6 tablespoons **crème
 fraîche**, to serve

Heat the oil in a large lidded saucepan. Add the white parts of the leeks and sweat, covered, shaking the pan from time to time, until softened but not browned. Add the potatoes and stir thoroughly.

Add the stock, milk and lavender flowers. Bring to the boil, cover and simmer for about 30 minutes or until the vegetables are tender. Add the green parts of the leeks for the last 10 minutes of cooking.

Remove the soup from the heat and leave to cool briefly. Remove the bundle of lavender and then blend until smooth. Adjust the seasoning if necessary and then reheat gently. Serve garnished with a spoonful of crème fraîche and a few lavender petals.

Carrot & ginger

Ginger gives this bright soup a delicious warmth, while the cream adds a cooling touch – just perfect!

Serves 4
Preparation time:
  10 minutes
Cooking time:
  15 minutes
Freezing:
  recommended

350 g (12 oz) **carrots**, peeled
  and sliced
600 ml (20 fl oz) **vegetable
  stock** (see page 8)
a knob of fresh **root ginger**,
  crushed
40 g (1½ oz) **butter**
2 **onions**, sliced
1 teaspoon **ground ginger**
1 teaspoon grated **orange
  zest**
2 tablespoons **orange juice**
salt and freshly ground
  black pepper
60 ml (2½ fl oz) **whipping
  cream**, whipped, to serve

Place the carrots, stock and fresh ginger in a saucepan. Bring to the boil and simmer for 15 minutes. Discard the ginger.

Meanwhile, melt the butter in a large lidded saucepan. Add the onions and sweat, covered, shaking the pan from time to time, until softened but not browned.

Stir in the ground ginger and orange zest and then add the cooked carrots and their cooking stock. Cover the pan, bring to the boil and simmer for 10 minutes.

Remove the soup from the heat and leave to cool briefly. Blend until smooth. Add the orange juice, adjust the seasoning if necessary and then reheat gently. Serve garnished with a spoonful of whipped cream.

Tomato & orange

This is a zingy summer soup that is ideal for an al-fresco dinner with friends. Use vine-ripened tomatoes for the best flavour.

Serves 6
Preparation time:
   10 minutes
Cooking time:
   20 minutes
Freezing:
   recommended

1 tablespoon **vegetable**
   or **olive oil**
1 **onion**, chopped
2 **celery sticks**, chopped
6 large **tomatoes**, quartered
   and de-seeded
2 **bay leaves**
850 ml (1½ pints) **chicken
   stock** (see page 9)
1 tablespoon **cornflour**
grated zest and juice of
   an **orange**
salt and freshly ground
   black pepper
1 teaspoon **caster sugar**
   or to taste
6 tablespoons **single cream**,
   to serve

Heat the oil in a large lidded saucepan. Add the onion and celery and sweat for 3–4 minutes, covered, shaking the pan from time to time, until softened but not browned.

Add the tomatoes, bay leaves and stock. Bring to the boil and simmer for 20 minutes or until the vegetables are tender.

Remove the soup from the heat and leave to cool briefly. Remove the bay leaves and then blend until smooth.

Blend the cornflour with a little water and stir into the soup, stirring all the time until completely mixed in. Reheat gently until slightly thickened.

Add the orange zest and juice. Adjust the seasoning if necessary and add sugar to taste.

Serve garnished with a swirl of cream.

Gazpacho

Serves 4
**Preparation and
  cooking time:
  30 minutes + chilling
Freezing:
  recommended**

6 tablespoons good-quality
  extra-virgin olive oil, plus
  extra to garnish
1 tablespoon finely chopped
  onion
2 fat **garlic cloves**, chopped
  finely and then crushed
½ large **cucumber**, chopped
2 **red peppers**, de-seeded
  and chopped roughly
1 **yellow pepper**, de-seeded
  and chopped roughly
7–8 very ripe **tomatoes**,
  chopped roughly
600 ml (20 fl oz) **chicken
  stock** (see page 9)
2 fat pinches **caster sugar**
2 teaspoons **tomato purée**
1–2 shakes **Tabasco** or
  chilli sauce
dash **white wine vinegar**
a large handful of fresh
  herbs, e.g. basil, tarragon
  or chervil
ice cubes, to serve

Heat a tablespoon of the oil in a lidded saucepan. Add the onion and garlic and sweat, covered, shaking the pan from time to time, until softened but not browned. Set this pan aside to go cold.

Set aside a small piece each of cucumber and red and yellow pepper. Put the rest of the cucumber and peppers into a food processor or blender with all the other ingredients except the ice cubes. Add the onion and garlic and whizz to a smoothish purée. Pour through a nylon sieve if liked and chill in the fridge until needed.

Serve in small bowls, with a few ice cubes in each bowl and garnished with a drizzle of olive oil and the reserved and chopped cucumber and red and yellow peppers scattered over.

Tofu & seafood

This is a delicious, clear Chinese soup, hence the use of chicken rather than fish stock.

Serves 4
**Preparation and
 cooking time:
 25 minutes**
**Freezing:
 not recommended**

12 large cooked **prawns**,
   shells removed, cut in
   half lengthways
225 g (8 oz) skinless,
   boneless **white fish**,
   thinly sliced
175 g (6 oz) **tofu**
1 teaspoon **cornflour**
1 teaspoon **sesame oil**
freshly ground **black pepper**
50 g (1¾ oz) **carrots**, peeled
   and sliced thinly
4 thin slices fresh **root
   ginger**
600 ml (20 fl oz) **chicken
   stock** (see Tip)
salt
2 **spring onions**, cut
   lengthways in 2.5 cm
   (1 inch) pieces, to garnish

Sprinkle the prawns, fish and tofu with the cornflour and oil and season with black pepper.

In a large lidded saucepan, cook the carrots and ginger in the stock for 10 minutes.

Add the prawns, fish and tofu and simmer for a further 2–3 minutes or until the fish is cooked.

Adjust the seasoning if necessary. Serve garnished with the spring onions.

Tip Make the stock as described on page 9 but omit the herbs and instead add a 2.5 cm (1 inch) grated piece of fresh root ginger and 1 tablespoon of soy sauce.

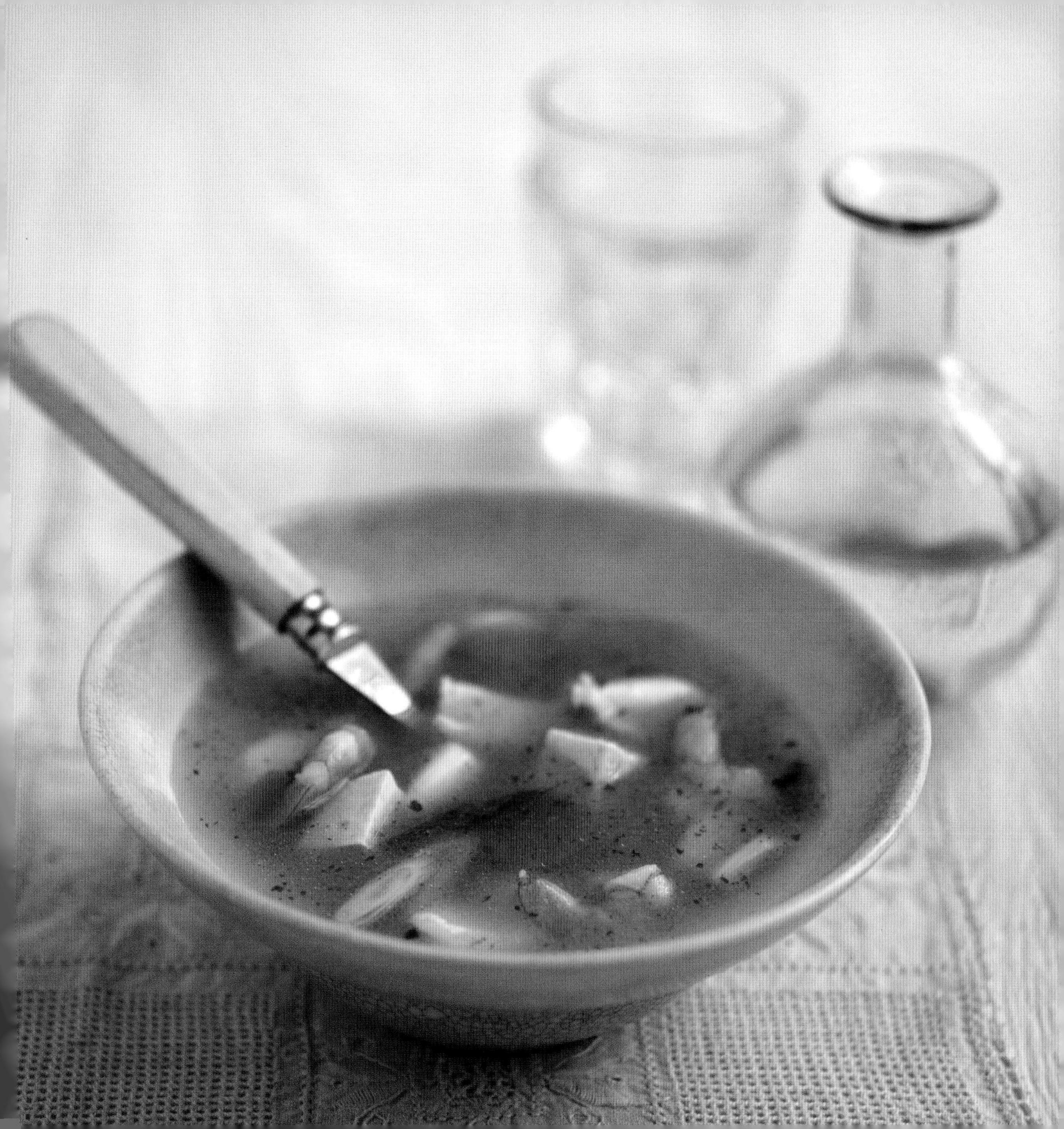

Leek & fennel

This soup has a delicate flavour and will make a delicious starter. Use only the whites of the leeks and well-rounded fennel.

Serves 4–5
Preparation time:
 10 minutes
Cooking time:
 20 minutes
Freezing:
 recommended

1 tablespoon **vegetable**
 or **olive oil**
25 g (1 oz) **butter**
900 g (2 lb) **leeks**, white
 parts only, sliced
1 large **fennel bulb**, sliced,
 leaves reserved to
 garnish
1 **garlic clove**, crushed
2 tablespoons **plain flour**
850 ml (1½ pints) **vegetable**
 or **chicken stock** (see
 pages 8 or 9)
salt and freshly ground
 black pepper

Heat the oil and butter in a large lidded saucepan. Add the leeks, fennel and garlic and sweat for 5 minutes, covered, shaking the pan from time to time, until softened but not browned.

Add the flour and stir well. Pour in the stock and make sure the flour is well blended. Bring to the boil, cover and simmer for 20 minutes.

Remove the soup from the heat and leave to cool briefly. Blend until smooth. Adjust the seasoning if necessary and then reheat gently. Serve garnished with the fennel leaves.

Celery & cashew nut

This is an unusual combination that you must try. It really is delicious and a great way of using up leftover celery.

Serves 4
Preparation time:
  10 minutes
Cooking time:
  15 minutes
Freezing:
  recommended

25 g (1 oz) **butter**
1 **onion**, chopped finely
1 **potato**, peeled and diced
½ head of **celery**, chopped,
  leaves reserved to
  garnish
80 g (3 oz) **cashew nuts**,
  chopped roughly
700 ml (1¼ pints) **vegetable
  stock** (see page 8)
15 g (½ oz) **plain flour**
450 ml (16 fl oz)
  semi-skimmed milk
salt and freshly ground
  black pepper

Gently melt the butter in a large lidded saucepan. Add the onion and potato and sweat for 5 minutes, covered, shaking the pan from time to time, until softened but not browned.

Stir in the chopped celery and cashew nuts and cook for a further 5 minutes.

Stir in the stock, bring to the boil and then reduce the heat and simmer for 15 minutes.

Blend the flour with a little of the milk, stir in the remainder of the milk and pour into the soup, stirring until the soup has thickened. Adjust the seasoning if necessary and reheat gently. Serve garnished with the reserved celery leaves.

Tarragon chicken

Chicken and tarragon is a classic combination that works perfectly together in this easy summery soup.

Serves 4–5
Preparation and
  cooking time:
   45 minutes
Freezing:
   not recommended

25 g (1 oz) **butter**
1 large **onion**, sliced finely
2 tablespoons **plain flour**
850 ml (1½ pints) **chicken
   stock** (see page 9)
finely grated zest and juice
   of ½ a **lemon**
225 g (8 oz) cooked,
   skinless, boneless
   chicken, cubed
1 tablespoon chopped
   fresh **tarragon**, plus extra
   sprigs, to garnish
150 ml (5 fl oz) **double cream**
salt and freshly ground
   white pepper

To garnish
finely sliced **lemon zest**
edible flowers (e.g. viola,
   borage)

Heat the butter in a large lidded saucepan. Add the onion and sweat for 5 minutes, covered, shaking the pan from time to time, until softened but not browned.

Add the flour and cook for 1 minute, stirring all the time. Gradually add the stock, making sure all the flour is well blended, and bring to the boil, stirring until thickened.

Add the lemon zest and juice, cover and simmer for 10 minutes. Add the chicken and tarragon and simmer for a further 5 minutes.

Remove the soup from the heat and leave to cool briefly. Stir in the cream. Adjust the seasoning if necessary and then reheat gently. Serve garnished with lemon zest and a few edible flowers.

Fish & tomato

Serves **4**
Preparation and
   cooking time:
   40 minutes
Freezing:
   recommended

2 **onions**, sliced
1 **leek**, white part only,
   sliced
3 fat **garlic cloves**, crushed
700 ml (1¼ pints) **fish stock**
   (see page 10)
1 **red pepper**, de-seeded
   and chopped
450 g (1 lb) **tomatoes**,
   skinned and chopped
1 tablespoon **tomato purée**
grated zest of ½ a **lemon**
juice of a **lemon**
1 small **cooking apple**,
   peeled, cored and
   chopped
3 tablespoons **dry white
   wine**
1 **bouquet garni** (see Tip)
450 g (1 lb) **white fish**, cut
   into bite-sized pieces
salt and freshly ground
   black pepper
3 tablespoons chopped
   fresh **parsley**, to garnish

Soften the onions, leek and garlic in a little of the stock in a large saucepan over a medium heat for 10 minutes.

Add the remaining stock, pepper, tomatoes, tomato purée, lemon zest and juice, apple and wine. Drop in the bouquet garni. Bring to the boil, reduce the heat and simmer for 10 minutes.

Remove the bouquet garni. Add the fish and gently simmer for 5 minutes. Adjust the seasoning if necessary. Serve scattered with the parsley.

Tip You can make your own bouquet garni of 1 fresh thyme sprig, 1 fresh marjoram sprig and 3 fresh parsley sprigs, tied with string or white cotton.

Broad bean

Provided broad beans are eaten young they have a delicate flavour.
They freeze well and are delicious with ham or bacon, hence this soup.

Serves 4
Preparation time:
 20 minutes
Cooking time:
 15 minutes
Freezing:
 recommended

25 g (1 oz) **butter**
1 **onion**, chopped
225 g (8 oz) podded and
 shelled fresh **broad beans**
175 g (6 oz) shelled fresh
 peas
425 ml (15 fl oz) **vegetable
 stock** (see page 8)
115 g (4¼ oz) lean **bacon**,
 chopped
300 ml (10 fl oz)
 semi-skimmed milk
salt and freshly ground
 black pepper

Melt the butter in a large lidded saucepan.
Add the onion and sweat, covered, shaking
the pan from time to time, until softened but
not browned.

Add the beans, peas and stock, with half
the bacon, and bring to the boil. Reduce the
heat and simmer for 15 minutes, or until the
vegetables are tender.

Meanwhile, dry fry the remaining bacon
in a non-stick pan until crispy.

Remove the soup from the heat and leave to
cool briefly. Blend half the soup until smooth
and then return to the pan with the unblended
soup. Add the milk and mix well. Adjust the
seasoning if necessary and then reheat gently.
Serve garnished with the crispy bacon.

Tip If fresh broad beans and peas are not
in season, use frozen.

Lettuce & lovage

If you have lovage growing in your garden, you'll be delighted with this recipe. Pick the young top leaves as the lower ones get very tough.

Serves 6
Preparation time:
   20 minutes
Cooking time:
   20 minutes
Freezing:
   recommended

25 g (1 oz) **butter**
175 g (6 oz) **spring onions**, chopped
250 g (9 oz) **potatoes**, peeled and chopped finely
1.5 kg (3 lb 5 oz) **iceberg lettuce**, chopped
600 ml (20 fl oz) **vegetable stock** (see page 8)
2 tablespoons **lemon juice**
25 g (1 oz) young **lovage leaves**, hard stems removed, chopped, plus tiny leaves, to garnish
425 ml (15 fl oz) **semi-skimmed milk**
300 ml (10 fl oz) **single cream**
salt and freshly ground **white pepper**

Melt the butter in a large lidded saucepan, and sweat the spring onions, covered, shaking the pan from time to time, until softened but not browned.

Add the potatoes, lettuce, stock and lemon juice and cover again. Bring to the boil and then reduce the heat and simmer gently for about 15 minutes, until the vegetables are tender.

Remove the soup from the heat and leave to cool briefly. Blend until smooth. Stir in the lovage and simmer gently, covered, for a further 5 minutes.

Stir in the milk and cream, adjust the seasoning if necessary and then reheat gently. Serve garnished with one or two baby lovage leaves.

Tip This recipe is based on one from the New Covent Garden Soup Company, though it's been altered slightly. They describe lovage as having an intense, celery-like flavour and say it was once called sea parsley. Our thanks to the company for a great recipe, which also uses up that flush of lettuce that comes to all of us in summer.

Green vegetable

Not only does this soup taste delicious but it uses up broccoli stems, the parts you normally discard, and asparagus stalks.

Serves 6
Preparation and
**   cooking time:**
**   40 minutes**
Freezing:
**   recommended**

50 g (1¾ oz) **butter**
225 g (8 oz) **asparagus**
**   stalks**
450 g (1 lb) **broccoli stems**
1 **leek**, sliced
4 **spring onions**, chopped
225 g (8 oz) shelled fresh or
   frozen **peas**
175 g (6 oz) **French** or **green**
**   beans**
1.1 litres (2 pints) **vegetable**
**   stoc**k (see page 8)
1 fresh **parsley sprig**
1 fresh **thyme sprig**
salt and freshly ground
**   black pepper**

Melt the butter in a large lidded saucepan. Add all the vegetables and sweat for approximately 10 minutes, covered, shaking the pan from time to time, until softened but not browned.

Add the stock and herbs, bring to the boil and simmer for 10–15 minutes until the vegetables are tender. Remove the thyme sprig.

Remove the soup from the heat and leave to cool briefly. Blend until smooth. Adjust the seasoning if necessary and then reheat gently before serving.

Lamb & leek

This is a modern version of Scotch broth or Welsh cawl. Use whatever vegetables you have at hand.

Serves 4
Preparation and
** cooking time: 1 hour**
Freezing:
** recommended**

25 g (1 oz) **butter**
225 g (8 oz) **neck fillet of**
  lamb, cubed
1 large **onion**, chopped
450 g (1 lb) mixed **root**
  vegetables (e.g. carrots,
  swede and parsnip),
  chopped
1.1 litres (2 pints) **chicken**
  stock (see page 9)
1 **potato**, peeled and
  chopped
225 g (8 oz) **leeks**, sliced
salt and freshly ground
  black pepper
juice of ½ a **lemon**, to taste
2 tablespoons chopped
  fresh **mint** or **parsley**

Melt the butter in a large lidded saucepan and sauté the lamb cubes until slightly brown. Remove from the pan.

Add the onion to the same pan and sweat for 5 minutes, covered, shaking the pan from time to time, until softened but not browned.

Return the lamb to the pan with the root vegetables. Add the stock, bring to the boil and simmer for 15 minutes.

Add the potato and simmer for a further 10 minutes. Add the leeks and simmer for a further 5–10 minutes.

Adjust the seasoning if necessary and add lemon juice to taste. Add the mint or parsley, reserving a little to sprinkle on top. Serve at once, sprinkled with the reserved chopped mint or parsley.

Fresh tomato & basil

Basil and tomatoes are a perfect flavour combination and the shallots give this soup a slight sweetness.

Serves 4–5
Preparation time:
 35 minutes
Cooking time:
 30 minutes
Freezing:
 recommended

50 g (1¾ oz) **butter** or
 2 tablespoons **vegetable**
 or **olive oil**
6 **shallots**, chopped
1 **garlic clove**, crushed
2 tablespoons **plain flour**
600 ml (20 fl oz) **chicken**
 stock (see page 9)
900 g (2 lb) **beef tomatoes**,
 skinned and chopped
 roughly
2 tablespoons **tomato purée**
3 tablespoons chopped
 fresh **basil**
salt and freshly ground
 black pepper

To garnish
4–5 slices **French bread**
olive oil
4–5 teaspoons **pesto**
tiny fresh **basil leaves**

Heat the butter or oil in a large lidded saucepan. Add the shallots and garlic and sweat for 3 minutes, covered, shaking the pan from time to time, until softened but not browned.

Add the flour and cook for 1 minute, stirring all the time. Gradually add the stock and bring to the boil, stirring all the time until thickened.

Stir in the tomatoes, tomato purée and basil, season well, cover and simmer for 30 minutes.

Meanwhile, fry the slices of bread in a little olive oil until golden. Remove with a slotted spoon and drain on kitchen towel. Keep warm.

Remove the soup from the heat and leave to cool briefly. Blend until smooth and then reheat gently. Spread the bread slices with the pesto. Serve garnished with the pesto breads, basil leaves and a drizzle of olive oil.

Courgette & mint

This is a great way to use up any gluts of courgettes from the garden. It can be served hot or cold, depending on your preference.

Serves 4
Preparation time:
  30 minutes + chilling (optional)
Cooking time:
  20 minutes
Freezing:
  recommended

25 g (1 oz) **butter**
1 **onion**, chopped
450 g (1 lb) **courgettes**, chopped
700 ml (1¼ pints) **vegetable** or **chicken stock** (see pages 8 or 9)
a handful of fresh **mint leaves**, plus extra sprigs, to garnish
salt and freshly ground **black pepper**
4 tablespoons **natural yogurt**, to serve

Melt the butter in a large lidded saucepan. Add the onion and sweat for 5 minutes, covered, shaking the pan from time to time, until softened but not browned. Add the courgettes and cook for a further 5 minutes.

Add the stock and half the mint leaves. Cover the pan, bring to the boil and simmer for 20 minutes.

Remove the soup from the heat and leave to cool briefly.

Add the remaining mint leaves and then blend until smooth. (Adding the mint in two batches preserves the flavour of the fresh herb in the finished soup.) Adjust the seasoning if necessary.

If serving hot, reheat gently. To serve cold, chill the soup for several hours. Serve garnished with a swirl of yogurt and a few mint leaves.

Sorrel & cucumber

Sorrel is not often used in cooking but is worth a try. It has a sharp, lemony taste, grows wild in some areas or may be bought at farmer's markets.

Serves 6
Preparation time:
 10 minutes + chilling
Cooking time:
 15 minutes
Freezing:
 recommended

1 generous bunch **sorrel leaves**, rinsed, torn up and stems discarded
1 thin **cucumber**, chopped
1.1 litres (2 pints) **chicken stock** (see page 9)
3 fat **spring onions**, chopped
1 **garlic clove**, sliced
150 ml (5 fl oz) **single cream**
salt and freshly ground **black pepper**

Simmer the sorrel, cucumber, stock, spring onions and garlic together in a large saucepan until the cucumber and spring onions are soft.

Remove the soup from the heat and leave to cool briefly. Blend until smooth.

Pour in the single cream, stir in well and adjust the seasoning if necessary. Chill for at least an hour, or until ready to serve. Serve cold, in small bowls.

Tip Try to find a thin cucumber as the fat ones have rather big seeds.

Roasted root vegetable

Roasting vegetables is well worth the effort as it gives the soup a different flavour. Vary the vegetables according to your taste and what is available.

Serves 6
Preparation time:
  35 minutes +
  30 minutes
  marinating
Cooking time: 1 hour
Freezing:
  recommended

450 g (1 lb) **celeriac**, peeled and cut into wedges
1 large **parsnip**, peeled and quartered lengthways
2 **carrots**, peeled and halved lengthways
8 **shallots**
1 large **sweet potato**, peeled and cut into eight
3 tablespoons **olive oil**
1 tablespoon fresh **thyme leaves**
salt and freshly **ground pepper**
850 ml (1½ pints) **vegetable stock** (see page 8)
6 tablespoons **single cream** or **natural yogurt**, to serve (optional)

Place all the vegetables in a large roasting tin, toss with the oil and sprinkle with the thyme and seasoning. Set aside to marinate for at least 30 minutes. Preheat the oven to 230°C/450°F/Gas Mark 8.

Roast the vegetables for 45 minutes, until the vegetables are beginning to brown.

Transfer to a large saucepan. Add the stock, bring to the boil and simmer for 15 minutes or until the vegetables are tender.

Remove the soup from the heat and leave to cool briefly. Blend until smooth, adding a little extra stock if necessary. Adjust the seasoning if necessary and then reheat gently.

Serve garnished with a swirl of cream or yogurt, if using.

Chilli bean

Feel free to add a little more or less chilli powder to suit your taste, and don't forget that the sausage will add spice too.

Serves 4–6
Preparation time:
 30 minutes
Cooking time:
 20 minutes
Freezing:
 recommended,
 without the sausage

1 tablespoon **vegetable**
 or **olive oil**
1 large **onion**, chopped
2 **carrots**, peeled and diced
425 g can **kidney beans**,
 drained and rinsed
1 teaspoon **chilli powder**
400 g carton **chopped**
 tomatoes
1 tablespoon **tomato purée**
600 ml (20 fl oz) **chicken**
 stock (see page 9)
salt and freshly ground
 black pepper
sliced **spicy sausage**, such
 as chorizo (optional)

Heat the oil in a large lidded saucepan. Add the onion and carrot and sweat, covered, shaking the pan from time to time, until softened but not browned.

Add the kidney beans and chilli powder. Cook for 1 minute. Add the tomatoes, tomato purée, stock and seasoning. Bring to the boil, reduce the heat, cover and simmer for 20 minutes.

Meanwhile, dry fry the sausage slices, if using, in a small non-stick pan until cooked.

Remove the soup from the heat and leave to cool briefly. Blend half the soup until coarsely chopped. Return to the remaining soup in the pan and reheat gently. Serve garnished with a few small slices of spicy sausage, if using.

Courgette & feta

Another great recipe to use up the late summer glut of courgettes. Teaming them with feta adds a lovely tanginess.

Serves 4
Preparation time:
  30 minutes
Cooking time:
  15–20 minutes
Freezing:
  recommended

2 tablespoons **olive oil**
1 large **onion**, chopped
2 **garlic cloves**, crushed
450 g (1 lb) **courgettes**, sliced
225 g (8 oz) **potatoes**, peeled and chopped
1 teaspoon chopped fresh **parsley**, plus extra, to garnish
700 ml (1¼ pints) **vegetable stock** (see page 8)
80 g (3 oz) **feta cheese**
salt and freshly ground **black pepper**

Heat the oil in a large lidded saucepan. Add the onion and garlic and sweat, covered, shaking the pan from time to time, until softened but not browned. Add the courgettes and potatoes and sweat for about 10 minutes.

Add the parsley and stock, bring to the boil and cook for 15–20 minutes or until the vegetables are softened.

Remove the soup from the heat and leave to cool briefly. Blend until smooth. Add the feta and, off the heat, stir until melted. Adjust the seasoning if necessary and then reheat gently. Serve scattered with the extra parsley.

Butterbean & celeriac

Butterbeans give this soup a creamy texture and complement the taste of the celeriac beautifully.

Serves 4
Preparation time:
  20 minutes +
  12 hours soaking
Cooking time:
  1¾ hours
Freezing:
  recommended

225 g (8 oz) dried
  butterbeans
1 litre (1¾ pints) **vegetable
  stock** (see page 8)
2 **onions**, chopped
1 **celeriac**, peeled and
  chopped
1 teaspoon **caraway seeds**
2 tablespoons chopped
  fresh **parsley**
600 ml (20 fl oz)
  semi-skimmed milk
salt and freshly ground
  black pepper

Place the butterbeans in a large bowl, cover with water and leave to soak for 12 hours.

Drain the beans, rinse well and transfer to a large saucepan. Pour in the stock, bring to the boil and cook for 1 hour.

Add the onions, celeriac, caraway seeds and parsley and simmer until the beans are tender (about another 45 minutes).

Remove the soup from the heat and leave to cool briefly. Blend until smooth and add the milk. Adjust the seasoning if necessary and then reheat gently. Serve.

Curried parsnip

Parsnips work wonderfully in many different soups. This one has just a touch of spice to warm you up on a cold day.

Serves 4
Preparation time:
  30 minutes
Cooking time:
  45 minutes
Freezing:
  recommended

1 tablespoon **vegetable**
  or **olive oil**
450 g (1 lb) **parsnips**, peeled
  and sliced
1 **onion**, chopped
1 teaspoon **curry powder**
700 ml (1¼ pints) **vegetable**
  stock (see page 8)
150 ml (5 fl oz)
  semi-skimmed milk
salt and freshly ground
  black pepper

To garnish
½ **onion**, sliced
1 tablespoon **olive oil**
4 tablespoons **natural**
  yogurt

Heat the oil in a large lidded saucepan. Add the parsnips and onion and sweat for 10 minutes, covered, shaking the pan from time to time, until softened but not browned.

Add the curry powder and cook for 2–3 minutes. Add the stock and milk and simmer for 45 minutes.

Meanwhile, fry the onion slices in the olive oil until light brown and crispy. Remove with a slotted spoon and set aside on kitchen towel to drain.

Remove the soup from the heat and leave to cool briefly. Blend until smooth. Adjust the seasoning if necessary and then reheat gently. Serve garnished with a spoonful of yogurt and a few crispy onion slices.

Creamy mussel

This is a complete meal in itself. Mussels are plentiful around the coast of north Wales and they are reputed to be some of the finest in this country.

Serves 4
**Preparation and
  cooking time: 1 hour**
**Freezing:
  not recommended**

2 kg (4½ lb) fresh **mussels**
300 ml (10 fl oz) **dry white
  wine**
2 **bay leaves**
6 whole **black peppercorns**
25 g (1 oz) **butter**
1 large **onion**, chopped
4 **garlic cloves**, crushed
300 ml (10 fl oz)
  semi-skimmed milk
salt and freshly ground
  black pepper
150 ml (5 fl oz) **single cream**
2 tablespoons chopped
  fresh **parsley**

Wash the mussels several times to remove any sand. Remove the 'beards' and discard any mussels that are broken or open.

Put the wine, bay leaves and peppercorns in a large lidded saucepan and bring to the boil. Add the mussels, cover and cook on a high heat for 3–4 minutes, shaking the pan to ensure all the mussels cook.

Discard any mussels that have not opened. Drain and reserve the liquor and remove most of the mussels from their shells, setting a few in their shells aside for garnish. Keep warm.

Melt the butter in the pan, add the onion and garlic and sweat, covered, shaking the pan from time to time, until softened but not browned.

Add the strained mussel liquor and the milk. Bring to the boil and then reduce the heat and leave to simmer until the onions and garlic are cooked. Adjust the seasoning if necessary.

Add the mussels, cream and parsley and reheat gently. Serve immediately, garnished with the reserved mussels in their shells.

Pumpkin & apple

This recipe works with any kind of pumpkin and is a lovely orange colour. It originally came from Australia, where pumpkins are used a lot for soup.

Serves 7–8
Preparation time:
  45 minutes
Cooking time:
  45 minutes
Freezing:
  recommended

80 g (3 oz) **butter**
2 large **onions**, sliced
1 kg (2 lb 4 oz) peeled and
  de-seeded **pumpkin flesh**,
  chopped
1 large **carrot**, peeled and
  chopped
1 large ripe **tomato**,
  chopped
1 **Granny Smith** or small
  cooking apple, peeled,
  cored and chopped
½ teaspoon **salt**
½ teaspoon **curry powder**
1.1 litres (2 pints) **vegetable
  stock** (see page 8)
freshly ground **black pepper**
3 tablespoons chopped
  fresh **mint**, to garnish

Melt the butter in a very large lidded saucepan, add the onions and sweat for at least 10 minutes, covered, shaking the pan from time to time, until softened but not browned.

Add everything else except the mint and stir well. Bring to the boil and then reduce the heat and leave to simmer for about 45 minutes or until all the vegetables are soft.

Remove the soup from the heat and leave to cool briefly. Blend until smooth (you will have to do this in batches). If the purée is too thick, add a little more water. Adjust the seasoning if necessary and then reheat gently. Serve scattered with the mint.

Split pea & ham

Peas and ham go beautifully together and this is an old favourite, enhanced by the addition of a little nutmeg.

Serves 4
Preparation time:
  45 minutes
Cooking time:
  45 minutes
Freezing:
  recommended

1 tablespoon **vegetable**
  or **olive oil**
1 large **onion**, chopped
1 **garlic clove**, crushed or
  chopped
a little freshly grated
  nutmeg
175 g (6 oz) **gammon**,
  chopped finely
175 g (6 oz) **dried split peas**
850 ml (1½ pints) **vegetable**
  or **chicken stock** (see
  pages 8 or 9)
½ teaspoon **caster sugar**
150 ml (5 fl oz) **single cream**
salt and freshly ground
  black pepper
chopped fresh **parsley**,
  to garnish

Heat the oil in a large lidded saucepan. Add the onion and garlic and sweat for 5 minutes, covered, shaking the pan from time to time, until softened but not browned.

Add the nutmeg and gammon and cook for a further 5 minutes.

Add the peas and stock. Bring to the boil, cover and simmer for 45 minutes or until the peas are mushy.

Stir in the sugar and cream and reheat gently. Adjust the seasoning if necessary. Serve sprinkled with the parsley.

Sweet potato & orange

This soup is refreshing, slightly sweet and a delightful colour; it's the ideal remedy for jaded appetites.

Serves 4
Preparation and
** cooking time:**
** 20 minutes**
Freezing:
** recommended**

25 g (1 oz) **butter**
1 **onion**, chopped
450 g (1 lb) **sweet potatoes**,
  peeled and grated
2 **celery sticks**, very finely
  chopped
850 ml (1½ pints) **vegetable**
  stock (see page 8)
2 fresh **thyme sprigs**
grated zest and juice of
  an **orange**
1 tablespoon chopped
  fresh **parsley**
salt and freshly ground
  black pepper

Melt the butter in a large lidded saucepan. Add the onion and sweat, covered, shaking the pan from time to time, until softened but not browned.

Add the sweet potatoes, celery, stock, thyme sprigs and orange zest. Bring to the boil and simmer for 10 minutes.

Remove the thyme sprigs and stir in the orange juice and parsley. Adjust the seasoning and then reheat gently if necessary. Serve.

Artichoke & spinach

This soup is made with knobbly Jerusalem artichokes. Don't miss out the hazelnuts – they are perfect with the soup.

Serves 4–5
Preparation time:
   45 minutes
Cooking time:
   20–25 minutes
Freezing:
   recommended

40 g (1½ oz) **butter**
1 small **onion**, sliced finely
350 g (12 oz) **Jerusalem artichokes**, peeled and sliced finely
600 ml (20 fl oz) **chicken stock** (see page 9)
175 g (6 oz) young **spinach leaves**, washed and tough stems discarded
salt and freshly ground **black pepper**
a little freshly grated **nutmeg**
300 ml (10 fl oz) **semi-skimmed milk**
80 g (3 oz) whole skinned **hazelnuts**, toasted, if wished, and slivered (see Tip), to garnish

Melt the butter in a large lidded saucepan. Add the onion and sweat, covered, shaking the pan from time to time, until softened but not browned.

Stir in the artichokes. Continue to sweat the vegetables for about 10 minutes.

Pour in the stock and bring to the boil. Reduce the heat and simmer gently, stirring often, for about 20–25 minutes or until the artichokes are really soft.

Add the spinach to the soup and remove the pan from the hob. (The spinach cooks enough in the residual heat of the pan and thus retains its colour.)

Leave to cool briefly and then blend until smooth. Adjust the seasoning if necessary and add a little grated nutmeg to taste. Stir in the milk and then reheat gently, without boiling. Serve garnished with the slivered hazelnuts.

Tip The best way to sliver the hazelnuts is with a slicing disc on a food processor.

French onion

Serves 6
Preparation and cooking time:
2½ hours
Freezing:
recommended, without the croûtes

115 g (4¼ oz) **butter**
2 kg (4 lb 8 oz) large **onions**, sliced as thinly as possible, slices cut into short lengths
1 tablespoon **plain flour**
1.5 litres (2¾ pints) best quality rich and jellied **beef stock**
150 ml (5 fl oz) **dry white wine**
a splash of **brandy** or **Calvados**
salt and freshly ground **black pepper**

Croûtes
1 **garlic clove**, crushed
1 teaspoon chopped fresh **parsley**
50 g (1¾ oz) **butter**, softened
1 small **baguette**, cut into 2.5 cm (1 inch) thick slices
175 g (6 oz) **Gruyère cheese**, grated finely

Melt the butter in a large lidded saucepan and add the onions. Stir well and then turn the heat to the lowest setting and cover the onions with a circle of dampened greaseproof paper. Allow the onions to soften for about 1 hour, stirring frequently.

Remove the paper and turn up the heat. Stir constantly and allow the onions to brown evenly.

Sprinkle the flour over the onions and stir and cook for a couple of minutes. Add the stock, a little at a time, stirring without stopping. As the soup thickens, add the wine and a splash of brandy or Calvados. Simmer for about 1 hour and adjust the seasoning if necessary. Preheat the oven to 220°C/425°F/Gas Mark 7.

To make the croûtes, add the garlic and parsley to the butter and beat well. Spread the slices of bread with the garlic butter and dip each buttered side into the grated cheese. Set the bread slices, cheesy-side up, on a baking sheet. Bake for about 10–15 minutes or until the cheese is bubbly and golden. Leave the bread to cool. If you wish, break the slices into bite-sized pieces. (This makes it much easier to eat.)

Warm six fairly large ovenproof soup bowls. Check that the soup is very hot and then divide it between the bowls. Place the cheesy toasts on the surface and sprinkle over the rest of the cheese. Place the bowls under a grill or in the oven and bake or grill until the cheese melts and bubbles. Serve at once.

Stilton & pear

This delicious recipe was given to us by farmer's wife, Liz Pexton. She and her husband have a farm near Driffield in East Yorkshire.

Serves 4
Preparation and cooking time: 1 hour
Freezing: recommended

15 g (½ oz) **butter**
1 **onion**, finely chopped
4 ripe **pears**, peeled, cored and chopped
850 ml (1½ pints) **chicken stock** (see page 9)
115 g (4¼ oz) **Stilton cheese**, crumbled
juice of ½ a **lemon**
salt and freshly ground **black pepper**
snipped fresh **chives**, to garnish

Melt the butter in a large lidded saucepan. Add the onion slowly and sweat, covered, shaking the pan from time to time, until softened but not browned.

Add the pears and stock. Simmer until the pears are tender (simmering time will depend on the type and ripeness of the pears).

Remove the soup from the heat and leave to cool briefly. Blend until smooth and then reheat gently.

Add the crumbled Stilton and stir until it melts. Add the lemon juice to taste and adjust the seasoning if necessary. Serve scattered with the snipped chives.

Carrot & coriander

A classic combination of flavours, this soup could also be cooked in the microwave (see Tip).

Serves 4
Preparation time:
  15 minutes
Cooking time:
  15 minutes
Freezing:
  recommended

25 g (1 oz) **butter**
1 **onion**, chopped
1 **garlic clove**, crushed
25 g (1 oz) **plain flour**
1 litre (1¾ pints) **chicken stock** (see page 9)
450 g (1 lb) **carrots**, peeled and grated
2 teaspoons chopped fresh **coriander**
salt and freshly ground **black pepper**
4 tablespoons **natural yogurt**, to serve

Melt the butter in a large lidded saucepan. Add the onion and garlic and sweat, covered, shaking the pan from time to time, until softened but not browned.

Blend in the flour and then add the stock gradually, stirring all the time over a low heat.

Add the carrots and coriander. Bring the soup to the boil and then let it simmer for 15 minutes.

Remove the pan from the heat and adjust the seasoning if necessary. Serve garnished with a swirl of yogurt.

Tip The general method for cooking soup in the microwave is to melt the butter first and then soften the onions in the butter on full power for 4 minutes. Allow another 4 minutes to sauté the vegetables. Add half the recommended quantity of boiling stock to the vegetables and cook on full power for 5 minutes. Stir and cook for a further 5 minutes or until the vegetables are cooked. Add the remaining boiling stock and continue as for conventional cooking.

Jerusalem artichoke

This soup is nearly saffron coloured, due to the carrots. It looks and tastes delicious and few people can guess what's in it.

Serves 4
Preparation time:
  10 minutes
Cooking time:
  30 minutes
Freezing:
  recommended

25 g (1 oz) **butter**
1 **onion**, chopped
2 **celery** sticks, chopped
1 litre (1¾ pints) **vegetable stock** (see page 8)
350 g (12 oz) **Jerusalem artichokes**, peeled and chopped
225 g (8 oz) **carrots**, peeled and chopped
salt and freshly ground **black pepper**

Melt the butter in a large lidded saucepan. Add the onion and celery and sweat for 5 minutes, covered, shaking the pan from time to time, until softened but not browned.

Add the stock and simmer for 20 minutes. Add the artichokes and carrots and cook for a further 10 minutes.

Remove the soup from the heat and leave to cool briefly. Blend until smooth. Adjust the seasoning if necessary and then reheat gently. Serve.

Tip Jerusalem artichokes discolour quickly so, as you peel each one, put it in a bowl of cold, salted water to keep the pale colour.

Beef with dumplings

Serves 4
Preparation and
cooking time:
60–75 minutes
Freezing:
recommended,
without dumplings

40 g (1½ oz) **butter**
400 g (14 oz) **stewing beef**,
    trimmed of fat and cubed
1 **onion**, chopped finely
1 litre (1¾ pints) **beef stock**
    (see page 11)
450 g (1 lb) mixed **root**
    vegetables, peeled and
    chopped
1 **leek**, sliced thinly
2 tablespoons chopped
    fresh **parsley**
salt and freshly ground
    black pepper

Dumplings
50 g (1¾ oz) **self-raising flour**
15 g (½ oz) **suet**
1 teaspoon chopped fresh
    parsley
fresh **thyme** leaves
salt and freshly ground
    black pepper
about 2 teaspoons
    semi-skimmed milk

Melt half the butter in a large lidded saucepan
and quickly fry the beef to seal and brown.
Remove with a slotted spoon.

Melt the remaining butter, add the onion and
fry until golden. Add the stock and return the
beef to the pan. Bring to the boil, reduce the
heat and leave to simmer for 10 minutes.

Add the mixed root vegetables, bring back
to the boil and then leave to simmer until
the beef and vegetables are tender, about
35–50 minutes.

Meanwhile, make the dumplings. Mix the
flour, suet, herbs and seasoning together in a
bowl. Blend together with the milk until you
have a soft but not sticky dough. Shape into
eight small balls by rolling in floury hands.

Add the leek and parsley to the soup and
simmer for a further 5 minutes.

Add the dumplings to the soup and cook for
5 minutes. Turn after 5 minutes and cook for
about 5 minutes more. The dumplings should
be light and fluffy when cooked.

Adjust the seasoning if necessary and serve
piping hot.

Tip Try adding 1–2 teaspoons of English
mustard for extra flavour.

Carrot & apple

Carrot is another vegetable that works so well with many other ingredients. This is a beautiful soup that goes down well throughout the year.

Serves 4
Preparation time:
  10 minutes
Cooking time:
  15 minutes
Freezing:
  recommended

1 tablespoon **olive oil**
25 g (1 oz) **butter**
1 **onion**, chopped
450 g (1 lb) **carrots**, peeled
  and chopped
225 g (8 oz) **apples**, peeled,
  cored and chopped
875 ml (1½ pints) **vegetable
  stock** (see page 8)
salt and freshly ground
  black pepper
a little freshly grated
  nutmeg, to serve

Heat the oil and butter in a large lidded saucepan until the butter has melted. Add the onion, carrots and apples and sweat for 5 minutes, covered, shaking the pan from time to time, until softened but not browned.

Add the stock and cook for 15 minutes, or until the vegetables and apples are tender.

Remove the soup from the heat and leave to cool briefly. Blend until smooth. Adjust the seasoning if necessary and then reheat gently. Serve sprinkled with a little nutmeg.

Hearty winter

This is a substantial soup that is simple to make but very tasty. It is also great for using up winter vegetables.

Serves 4
Preparation time:
  25 minutes
Cooking time:
  30 minutes
Freezing:
  recommended

600 ml (20 fl oz) **vegetable**
  or **chicken stock** (see
  pages 8 or 9)
1 **potato**, peeled and diced
1 **onion**, diced
1 large **carrot**, peeled and
  diced
1 **tomato**, skinned (see page
  36) and chopped roughly
1 **turnip** or ½ a **swede**,
  peeled and diced
1 small **parsnip**, peeled and
  diced
1 tablespoon **tomato purée**
2 tablespoons chopped
  fresh **parsley**
salt and freshly ground
  black pepper

Put the stock into a large lidded saucepan and bring to the boil. Add the vegetables, together with the tomato purée.

When the stock is just at the boil, reduce the heat, cover and simmer gently for about 30 minutes or until the vegetables are tender. Stir in most of the parsley and adjust the seasoning if necessary.

Serve this soup as it is or remove from the heat, leave to cool briefly and blend until smooth. Reheat gently if necessary and serve scattered with the remaining parsley.

Chicken pesto

This is a substantial soup, which can be served as a main course. It is colourful, satisfying and there is only one pan to wash at the end!

Serves 4–6
Preparation and cooking time:
30 minutes
Freezing:
recommended, without pesto

1 tablespoon **vegetable or olive oil**
2 **chicken leg portions**, halved
1 large **onion**, chopped
2 tablespoons **plain flour**
1 litre (1¾ pints) **chicken stock** (see page 9)
1 tablespoon **tomato purée**
salt and freshly ground **black pepper**
80 g (3 oz) **baby pasta shapes**
225 g (8 oz) **broccoli**, cut into small florets, stalk sliced
115 g (4¼ oz) **French beans**, sliced thickly
2 tablespoons **pesto**, plus extra to serve

Heat the oil in a large saucepan and fry the chicken pieces on both sides until browned, about 10 minutes.

Add the onion and continue to fry for a further 10 minutes, stirring occasionally. Stir in the flour to combine with the juices.

Add the stock and tomato purée and season. Stir well to make sure the flour is completely blended, bring to the boil, cover and simmer for 15 minutes. Stir in the pasta and cook for 5 minutes.

Add the broccoli and French beans and cook for a few more minutes, until the vegetables and pasta are tender but not soft.

Remove the chicken from the pan. When cool enough to handle, discard the skin and bones and cut the meat into thin strips. Return to the pan, together with the pesto.

Stir well, reheat gently and serve, with additional pesto on the side so that your guests can add it to the bowls themselves.

Winter lentil & mint

This is a lovely soup for a cold wintery day, served piping hot. Dried mint loses its flavour quickly, so this recipe uses mint sauce from a jar.

Serves 4–6
Preparation time:
10 minutes
Cooking time:
30 minutes
Freezing:
recommended, before blending

1 tablespoon **vegetable** or **olive oil**
a knob of **butter**
1 **onion**, sliced finely
1 small **garlic clove**, sliced
2 tablespoons **tomato purée**
115 g (4¼ oz) **Puy lentils**
1.1 litres (2 pints) **vegetable** or **chicken stock** (see pages 8 or 9)
40 g (1½ oz) **bulgar wheat**
2 teaspoons **lemon juice**
2 heaped teaspoons **mint sauce** or 2 tablespoons chopped **fresh mint**
salt and freshly ground **black pepper**

Melt the oil and butter in a large lidded saucepan. Add the onion and garlic and sweat, covered, shaking the pan from time to time, until softened but not browned.

Add the tomato purée and lentils and stir so that all is well mixed. Add the stock and bring to the boil. Reduce the heat and leave to simmer for about 30 minutes, or until the lentils are soft.

Remove the soup from the heat and leave to cool briefly. Blend half the soup until smooth.

Return the blended soup to the pan and stir in the bulgar wheat, lemon juice and mint sauce or fresh mint. Adjust the seasoning if necessary and simmer for another 2 minutes. Serve piping hot.

Chestnut & cranberry

This is a recipe developed to use up Christmas leftovers! Sweet chestnuts and sharp cranberries combine to give a delicious, satisfying soup.

Serves 6
Preparation and cooking time:
  25 minutes
Freezing:
  recommended, after blending

6 **shallots**, chopped
3 **celery sticks**, chopped
1 litre (1¾ pints) **vegetable stock** (see page 8)
a fresh **thyme sprig**, plus a few extra thyme leaves, to garnish
450 g (1 lb) peeled, cooked **chestnuts**
115 g (4¼ oz) fresh **cranberries**
4 tablespoons **port**
2 tablespoons **lemon juice**
salt and freshly ground **black pepper**
150 ml (5 fl oz) **double cream**, to garnish

Put the shallots, celery and 2 tablespoons of stock in a large saucepan and soften the vegetables over a low heat until transparent.

Add the remaining stock and thyme. Bring to the boil, reduce the heat and leave to simmer for 10 minutes. Add the chestnuts and cranberries. Bring to the boil and simmer for a further 5 minutes. Remove 4 tablespoons of drained vegetables, chestnuts and cranberries for the garnish, crumbling any large pieces of chestnut.

Remove the soup from the heat and leave to cool briefly. Blend until smooth. Stir in the port and lemon juice to taste, adjust the seasoning if necessary and then reheat gently.

Serve topped with a swirl of cream, the reserved garnish ingredients and a few thyme leaves.

Tips Make this at any time of year using frozen cranberries and canned or vacuum-packed chestnuts or unsweetened chestnut purée.

To skin fresh chestnuts, puncture each chestnut with a fork, put in a pan of boiling water and keep at simmering point. Remove a few chestnuts at a time and plunge into cold water. Skin with the help of a vegetable knife.

Chick pea & tomato

We all say at one time or another, 'What on earth is there to eat?' This soup is a good answer, as it can be made mostly from store cupboard ingredients.

Serves 4
Preparation time:
10 minutes
Cooking time:
30 minutes
Freezing:
recommended

2 tablespoons **sunflower oil**
1 **red onion**, chopped
2 **garlic cloves**, crushed
2 teaspoons **cumin seeds**
1 teaspoon **mild curry powder**
2 x 400 g cans **chopped tomatoes**
175 g (6 oz) **carrots**, peeled and diced
50 g (1¾ oz) **red lentils**
finely grated zest and juice of an **orange**
425 g can **chick peas**, drained and rinsed
salt and freshly ground **black pepper**
Croûtons, to garnish (see page 30)

Heat the oil in a large lidded saucepan. Add the onion, garlic, cumin seeds and curry powder and sweat for 5 minutes, covered, shaking the pan from time to time, until softened but not browned.

Add the tomatoes, carrots, lentils and orange zest. Make up the orange juice to 600 ml (20 fl oz) with water and stir into the soup. Bring to the boil, cover and simmer for 30 minutes until the carrots are tender.

Remove the soup from the heat and leave to cool briefly. Blend until smooth or use a potato masher to give fairly coarse texture. Add the chick peas and adjust the seasoning if necessary. Reheat gently and serve scattered with the croûtons.

Leek & broccoli.

A delicious winter soup that is full of green goodness. It's very quick to make, too – perfect at the end of a busy day.

Serves 4
Preparation time:
 10 minutes
Cooking time:
 15 minutes
Freezing:
 not recommended

50 g (1¾ oz) **butter**
450 g (1 lb) **leeks**, sliced
  thinly
225 g (8 oz) **broccoli**,
  chopped
1 **garlic clove**, crushed
  (optional)
2 tablespoons **plain flour**
600 ml (20 fl oz) **vegetable** or
  chicken stock (see pages
  8 or 9)
600 ml (20 fl oz)
  semi-skimmed milk
salt and freshly ground
  black pepper
4 tablespoons **single cream**
  or **crème fraîche**, to
  garnish

Melt the butter in a large lidded saucepan. Add the leeks, broccoli and garlic (if using) and sweat for 5 minutes, covered, shaking the pan from time to time, until softened but not browned.

Sprinkle in the flour, stir well and cook briefly. Add the stock, make sure all the flour is blended and bring to the boil. Reduce the heat and cook for 15 minutes, or until the vegetables are softened.

Remove the soup from the heat and leave to cool briefly. Blend until smooth if you wish, or leave it chunky. Add the milk, adjust the seasoning if necessary and then reheat gently. Serve garnished with a swirl of cream or crème fraîche.

Watercress & almond

Serves **5–6**
**Preparation and
cooking time:
20 minutes + 2 hours
chilling**
Freezing:
**recommended, after
blending**

1 tablespoon **vegetable
or olive oil**
1 small **onion**, chopped
finely
850 ml (1½ pints) **vegetable
or chicken stock** (see
pages 8 or 9)
2 tablespoons **ground
almonds**
2 bunches **watercress**,
thoroughly washed and
dried
juice of an **orange**
1 teaspoon grated **orange
zest**, plus extra, to garnish
150 ml (5 fl oz)
semi-skimmed milk
150 ml (5 fl oz) **single cream**
salt and freshly ground
black pepper
a small handful of **toasted
flaked almonds**, to
garnish

Heat the oil in a large lidded saucepan. Add the onion and sweat, covered, shaking the pan from time to time, until softened but not browned.

Add the stock, ground almonds and watercress. Simmer for just a few minutes. Stir in the orange juice and zest and simmer for another 3–4 minutes.

Remove the soup from the heat and leave to cool briefly. Blend until smooth. Stir in the milk and cream, allow the soup to cool and then refrigerate for 2 hours – it should be chilled but not icy.

Adjust the seasoning if necessary and serve in small bowls. Sprinkle a few almonds on top of each bowl, along with a little orange zest.

Vegetable chowder

Chowders are usually made with milk or cream and often contain seafood. Here, we have used winter vegetables for a tasty, satisfying soup.

Serves 4
**Preparation and
  cooking time:
  50 minutes**
**Freezing:
  recommended**

1 tablespoon **vegetable**
  or **olive oil**
1 large **onion**, chopped
225 g (8 oz) **potatoes**, peeled
  and chopped
225 g (8 oz) **carrots**, peeled
  and diced
3 **celery sticks**, diced
400 g can **chopped
  tomatoes**
115 g (4¼ oz) **macaroni**
425 ml (15 fl oz) **vegetable
  stock** (see page 8)
1 **bay leaf**
1 teaspoon dried **oregano**
300 ml (10 fl oz)
  semi-skimmed milk
salt and freshly ground
  black pepper
chopped fresh **parsley**,
  to garnish

Heat the oil in a large lidded saucepan. Add the onion, potatoes, carrots and celery and sweat for 5 minutes, covered, shaking the pan from time to time, until softened but not browned.

Add the tomatoes, macaroni, stock and herbs. Bring to the boil, reduce the heat, cover and simmer for 15 minutes.

Stir in the milk and adjust the seasoning if necessary. Discard the bay leaf and bring back to the boil. Serve scattered with the parsley.

Sweet potato & red pepper

The pinkish colour of the sweet potato and deep red of the pepper give this soup a delightful colour, and the coconut milk adds a tropical flavour.

Serves 4
Preparation time:
 35 minutes
Cooking time:
 20 minutes
Freezing:
 recommended

25 g (1 oz) **butter**
1 **onion**, chopped
1 **garlic clove**, crushed
1 tablespoon **ground coriander**
450 g (1 lb) **sweet potatoes**, diced, plus extra to garnish
2 **red peppers**, de-seeded and chopped
700 ml (1¼ pints) **vegetable stock** (see page 8)
400 g can **coconut milk**
vegetable oil, for frying

Melt the butter in a large lidded saucepan. Add the onion and garlic and sweat, covered, shaking the pan from time to time, until softened but not browned.

Stir in the ground coriander and cook for 2 minutes. Add the sweet potatoes and red peppers and cook for 5 minutes. Pour the vegetable stock over, bring to the boil, cover and simmer for 20 minutes.

Meanwhile, cut the extra sweet potato into thin slices (use a mandolin if you have one). Heat about 1 cm (½ inch) of vegetable oil in a frying pan and fry the slices in batches until golden and crisp. Remove with a slotted spoon and place on kitchen towel to dry.

Remove the soup from the heat and leave to cool briefly. Blend until smooth. Add the coconut milk and then reheat gently. Serve at once, garnished with the sweet potato crisps.

Tip If you can't find coconut milk, use 100 g (3½ oz) of creamed coconut, chopped, and increase the amount of stock by about 150 ml (5 fl oz).

Cabbage & bacon

This is a modern version of boiled bacon and cabbage, a perennial favourite. It is quick and easy to make, looks good and tastes even better!

Serves 4
Preparation and cooking time:
  20 minutes
Freezing:
  recommended

25 g (1 oz) **butter**
2 **onions**, chopped finely
6 rindless **bacon rashers**, chopped
1 litre (1¾ pints) **vegetable stock** (see page 8)
450 g (1 lb) **Savoy cabbage**, sliced thinly
salt and freshly ground **black pepper**

Melt the butter in a large lidded saucepan. Add the onions and sweat, covered, shaking the pan from time to time, until softened but not browned.

Add the bacon and increase the heat. Stirring continuously, cook until the onions and bacon begin to brown. Add the stock and bring to the boil.

Add the cabbage. Cook until the cabbage is tender but still firm, approximately 5 minutes. Adjust the seasoning if necessary before serving.

Bean with guacamole salsa

Serves 6
**Preparation and
  cooking time:**
  50 minutes
Freezing:
  **recommended,
  without salsa**

2 tablespoons **vegetable**
  or **olive oil**
2 **onions**, chopped
4 fat **garlic cloves**, crushed
2 teaspoons **ground cumin**
a pinch of **cayenne pepper**
1 tablespoon **paprika**
1 tablespoon **tomato purée**
2 tablespoons **ground
  coriander**
400 g can **chopped
  tomatoes**
400 g can **red kidney beans**,
  drained and rinsed
1 litre (1¾ pints) **vegetable
  stock** (see page 8)
salt and freshly ground
  black pepper

Guacamole salsa
2 **avocados**
1 **green chilli**
1 **red onion**
1 tablespoon chopped fresh
  coriander
juice of a **lime**

Heat the oil in a large lidded saucepan.
Add the onions and garlic and sweat, covered,
shaking the pan from time to time, until
softened but not browned.

Add all the remaining soup ingredients, bring
to the boil and simmer over a low heat for
20 minutes.

Meanwhile, peel and stone the avocados and
chop the flesh roughly. De-seed and finely chop
the chilli and finely chop the onion. Mix all the
salsa ingredients together.

Remove the soup from the heat and leave to
cool briefly. Blend until smooth. Adjust the
seasoning if necessary and then reheat gently.

Serve garnished with a little of the salsa in
the middle of each bowl.

Broccoli & Stilton

Perfect for a Boxing Day lunch, this is a great way to use up leftover Stilton, a classic Christmas cheese.

Serves 6
Preparation and
** cooking time:**
** 50 minutes**
Freezing:
** not recommended**

1 tablespoon **vegetable**
  or **olive oil**
1 **onion**, chopped
2 large **potatoes**, peeled
  and chopped
1.1 litres (2 pints) **vegetable**
  or **chicken stock** (see
  pages 8 or 9)
350 g (12 oz) **broccoli**,
  chopped roughly
80 g (3 oz) **Stilton cheese**,
  crumbled, plus a little
  extra, to garnish
150 ml (5 fl oz)
  semi-skimmed milk
juice of ½ a **lemon**
salt and freshly ground
  black pepper

Heat the oil in a large lidded saucepan. Add the onion and sweat, covered, shaking the pan from time to time, until softened but not browned.

Add the potatoes and stock and bring to the boil. Simmer for 10 minutes. Add the broccoli and cook for a further 10 minutes.

Remove the soup from the heat and leave to cool briefly. Blend until smooth or just mash the vegetables roughly if you prefer a chunkier texture.

Add the Stilton and milk, and add lemon juice to taste. Adjust the seasoning if necessary and reheat gently. Serve garnished with a little crumbled Stilton.

Scotch broth

Start this recipe the day before you need it, so that you can chill the soup overnight and remove every scrap of fat from the top for the best flavour.

Serves 6
Preparation time:
 20 minutes +
 overnight chilling
Cooking time:
 3 hours 20 minutes
Freezing:
 recommended

900 g (2 lb) **scrag end of lamb**, trimmed of all excess fat
115 g (4¼ oz) **pearl barley**
1 **bouquet garni**
salt and freshly ground **black pepper**
1 **onion**, chopped finely
1 small **white turnip**, peeled and diced
2 large **carrots**, peeled and diced, or 2 tablespoons diced **swede**
115 g (4¼ oz) **cabbage**, shredded
1 large **leek**, sliced
1 tablespoon finely chopped fresh **parsley**, to garnish (optional)

Place the lamb in a large heavy-based saucepan and add the pearl barley, bouquet garni and 2 litres (3½ pints) of water. Season. Bring the pan slowly to the boil. Skim any white scum from the surface, cover and simmer for 2 hours.

Add the onion, turnip and carrot or swede to the soup and continue to simmer for 1 hour.

Remove the lamb from the soup with a slotted spoon and leave it to stand until it is cool enough to handle. Strip the meat from the bones and cut into small pieces. Cover and set aside in the fridge.

Allow the soup to cool and then chill it overnight so that the fat rises and sets on the surface. Remove the fat and then bring the soup back up to the boil.

Return the lamb to the soup and add the cabbage and leek. Top up with extra water if needed. Bring back to the boil, adjust the seasoning if necessary and simmer for another 20 minutes. Serve scattered with the parsley, if using.

Index